THREE STORIES
AND TEN POEMS

THREE STORIES AND TEN POEMS

Ernest Hemingway

DOVER PUBLICATIONS, INC.
MINEOLA, NEW YORK

DOVER THRIFT EDITIONS

GENERAL EDITOR: SUSAN L. RATTINER
EDITOR OF THIS VOLUME: TERRI ANN GEUS

Copyright

Copyright © 2019 by Dover Publications, Inc.
All rights reserved.

Bibliographical Note

This Dover edition, first published in 2019, is an unabridged republication of the work originally published by the Contact Publishing Co., Paris, in 1923. A new introductory Note has been specially prepared for this edition.

Library of Congress Cataloging-in-Publication Data

Names: Hemingway, Ernest, 1899–1961, author.
Title: Three stories and ten poems / Ernest Hemingway.
Description: Mineola, NY: Dover Publications, 2019. | Series: Dover thrift editions
Identifiers: LCCN 2018029915| ISBN 9780486828312 (paperback) | ISBN 048682831X (paperback)
Subjects: | BISAC: LITERARY COLLECTIONS / American / General.
Classification: LCC PS3515.E37 A6 2019 | DDC 813/.52—dc23
LC record available at https://lccn.loc.gov/2018029915

Manufactured in the United States by LSC Communications
82831X02   2019
www.doverpublications.com

THIS BOOK
IS FOR HADLEY

Note

ERNEST MILLER HEMINGWAY was born in Oak Park, Illinois, on July 21, 1899, the second of five children born to Grace Hall Hemingway, a musician, and Clarence Edmonds Hemingway, a doctor. At the age of seventeen, Hemingway began his writing career as a journalist for *The Kansas City Star*. He was there just a few months before enlisting to serve as an ambulance driver in Italy with the American Red Cross during World War I, where he was seriously wounded. Hemingway spent six months in the hospital and returned home to Illinois in 1918 with the Silver Medal of Valor from the Italian government. His wartime experiences would later serve as inspiration for *A Farewell to Arms*, which was published in 1929. Likewise, Hemingway's experiences as a reporter for the North American Newspaper Alliance during the Spanish Civil War served as the background for his novel *For Whom the Bell Tolls* in 1940, which was mostly written in Havana, Cuba, while Hemingway was in residence there.

After returning home from his injury in World War I, Hemingway worked for Canadian and American newspapers. It was while he was a correspondent for the *Toronto Star* that the author met the first of his four wives, Hadley Richardson, and moved to Paris. Here they spent much time in the company of other expatriate writers, such as F. Scott Fitzgerald, Gertrude Stein, and Ezra Pound. Based on real people and events from the author's life, his "modernist" novel *The Sun Also Rises* (1926) was written and published based on three trips that Hemingway had taken to Pamplona, Spain, with Hadley Richardson and others. During the twenty-month time span that the couple lived in Paris, Hemingway also penned more than eighty stories for the Toronto newspaper, on subjects ranging from fishing and bullfighting to travel and war.

In September 1923, the couple left Paris to return to Toronto. It is during this time when *Three Stories and Ten Poems*—Hemingway's first book—was published. Only three hundred copies of the first edition were originally printed. This initial book led to the author's being recognized as one of the major figures of the Modernist movement, even though the subject matter of the first of the three stories, "Up in Michigan," was considered deplorable by some close to Hemingway (including Gertrude Stein and the author's parents) at the time of its printing. While Hemingway's works may still seem crude to some readers, for others, his simple and direct style is exactly why Hemingway has been a favorite writer for so many people. Six of the poems contained in the book, "Mitraigliatrice" (originally spelled "Mitrailliatrice"), "Oily Weather," "Roosevelt," "Riparto d'Assalto," "Champs d'Honneur," and "Chapter Heading," had originally appeared in *Poetry: A Magazine of Verse*: Volume XXI, October–March, 1922–23, which was printed in Chicago.

Among Hemingway's later works—perhaps the most well-known—is the short novel he wrote while living in Cuba, *The Old Man and the Sea*, published in 1952. This story of an aging Cuban fisherman and his struggles with a giant marlin and the elements was the last fictional work that was published during Hemingway's lifetime. The Nobel Prize in Literature was awarded to Ernest Hemingway in 1954, citing "his mastery of the art of narrative . . . and for the influence that he has exerted on contemporary style."

★ ★ ★

Ernest Hemingway was married four times and had three sons. He and his wife, Hadley Richardson, had one son, John Hadley Nicanor "Jack" Richardson, who was born in Toronto in 1923, the same year as the first printing of this book. His son Patrick was born in 1928 and his son Gregory was born in 1931; both were the children of Hemingway's second wife, Pauline Pfeiffer. War correspondent Martha Gellhorn was married to Hemingway from 1940 to 1945. Fellow journalist and author Mary Welsh Hemingway met the author in London while covering World War II. They were married in Cuba in 1946 and remained married until Hemingway's death by suicide in their home in Ketchum, Idaho, in 1961.

Contents

THREE STORIES

UP IN MICHIGAN

UP IN MICHIGAN

Jim Gilmore came to Hortons Bay from Canada. He bought the blacksmith shop from old man Horton. Jim was short and dark with big mustaches and big hands. He was a good horse-shoer and did not look much like a blacksmith even with his leather apron on. He lived upstairs above the blacksmith shop and took his meals at A. J. Smith's.

Liz Coates worked for Smith's. Mrs. Smith, who was a very large clean woman, said Liz Coates was the neatest girl she'd ever seen. Liz had good legs and always wore clean gingham aprons and Jim noticed that her hair was always neat behind. He liked her face because it was so jolly but he never thought about her.

Liz liked Jim very much. She liked it the way he walked over from the shop and often went to the kitchen door to watch for him to start down the road. She liked it about his mustache. She liked it about how white his teeth were when he smiled. She liked it very much that he didn't look like a blacksmith. She liked it how much A. J. Smith and Mrs. Smith liked Jim. One day she found that she liked it the way the hair was black on his arms and how white they were above the tanned line when he washed up in the washbasin outside the house. Liking that made her feel funny.

Hortons Bay, the town, was only five houses on the main road between Boyne City and Charlevoix. There was the

3

general store and post office with a high false front and maybe a wagon hitched out in front, Smith's house, Stroud's house, Fox's house, Horton's house and Van Hoosen's house. The houses were in a big grove of elm trees and the road was very sandy. There was farming country and timber each way up the road. Up the road a ways was the Methodist church and down the road the other direction was the township school. The blacksmith shop was painted red and faced the school.

A steep sandy road ran down the hill to the bay through the timber. From Smith's back door you could look out across the woods that ran down to the lake and across the bay. It was very beautiful in the spring and summer, the bay blue and bright and usually whitecaps on the lake out beyond the point from the breeze blowing from Charlevoix and Lake Michigan. From Smith's back door Liz could see ore barges way out in the lake going toward Boyne City. When she looked at them they didn't seem to be moving at all but if she went in and dried some more dishes and then came out again they would be out of sight beyond the point.

All the time now Liz was thinking about Jim Gilmore. He didn't seem to notice her much. He talked about the shop to A. J. Smith and about the Republican Party and about James G. Blaine. In the evenings he read the Toledo Blade and the Grand Rapids paper by the lamp in the front room or went out spearing fish in the bay with a jacklight with A. J. Smith. In the fall he and Smith and Charley Wyman took a wagon and tent, grub, axes, their rifles and two dogs and went on a trip to the pine plains beyond Vanderbilt deer hunting. Liz and Mrs. Smith were cooking for four days for them before they started. Liz wanted to make something special for Jim to take but she didn't finally because she was afraid to ask Mrs. Smith for the eggs and flour and afraid if she bought them Mrs. Smith would catch her cooking. It would have been all right with Mrs. Smith but Liz was afraid.

All the time Jim was gone on the deer hunting trip Liz thought about him. It was awful while he was gone. She couldn't sleep well from thinking about him but she discovered it was fun to think about him too. If she let herself go it was better. The night before they were to come back she didn't sleep at all, that is she didn't think she slept because it was all mixed up in a dream about not sleeping and really not sleeping. When she saw the wagon coming down the road she felt weak and sick sort of inside. She couldn't wait till she saw Jim and it seemed as though everything would be all right when he came. The wagon stopped outside under the big elm and Mrs. Smith and Liz went out. All the men had beards and there were three deer in the back of the wagon, their thin legs sticking stiff over the edge of the wagon box. Mrs. Smith kissed Alonzo and he hugged her. Jim said "Hello Liz." and grinned. Liz hadn't known just what would happen when Jim got back but she was sure it would be something. Nothing had happened. The men were just home that was all. Jim pulled the burlap sacks off the deer and Liz looked at them. One was a big buck. It was stiff and hard to lift out of the wagon.

"Did you shoot it Jim?" Liz asked.

"Yeah. Aint it a beauty?" Jim got it onto his back to carry to the smokehouse.

That night Charley Wyman stayed to supper at Smith's. It was too late to get back to Charlevoix. The men washed up and waited in the front room for supper.

"Aint there something left in that crock Jimmy?" A. J. Smith asked and Jim went out to the wagon in the barn and fetched in the jug of whiskey the men had taken hunting with them. It was a four gallon jug and there was quite a little slopped back

and forth in the bottom. Jim took a long pull on his way back
to the house. It was hard to lift such a big jug up to drink out
of it. Some of the whiskey ran down on his shirt front. The two
men smiled when Jim came in with the jug. A. J. Smith sent
for glasses and Liz brought them. A. J. poured out three big
shots.

"Well here's looking at you A. J." said Charley Wyman.

"That damn big buck Jimmy." said A. J.

"Here's all the ones we missed A. J." said Jim and downed
his liquor.

"Tastes good to a man."

"Nothing like it this time of year for what ails you."

"How about another boys?"

"Here's how A. J."

"Down the creek boys."

"Here's to next year."

Jim began to feel great. He loved the taste and the feel of
whisky. He was glad to be back to a comfortable bed and warm
food and the shop. He had another drink. The men came in to
supper feeling hilarious but acting very respectable. Liz sat at
the table after she put on the food and ate with the family. It
was a good dinner. The men ate seriously. After supper they
went into the front room again and Liz cleaned off with Mrs.
Smith. Then Mrs. Smith went up stairs and pretty soon Smith
came out and went up stairs too. Jim and Charley were still in
the front room. Liz was sitting in the kitchen next to the stove
pretending to read a book and thinking about Jim. She didn't
want to go to bed yet because she knew Jim would be coming
out and she wanted to see him as he went out so she could take
the way he looked up to bed with her.

She was thinking about him hard and then Jim came out. His
eyes were shining and his hair was a little rumpled. Liz looked
down at her book. Jim came over back of her chair and stood

there and she could feel him breathing and then he put his arms around her. Her breasts felt plump and firm and the nipples were erect under his hands. Liz was terribly frightened, no one had ever touched her, but she thought, "He's come to me finally. He's really come."

She held herself stiff because she was so frightened and did not know anything else to do and then Jim held her tight against the chair and kissed her. It was such a sharp, aching, hurting feeling that she thought she couldn't stand it. She felt Jim right through the back of the chair and she couldn't stand it and then something clicked inside of her and the feeling was warmer and softer. Jim held her tight hard against the chair and she wanted it now and Jim whispered, "Come on for a walk."

Liz took her coat off the peg on the kitchen wall and they went out the door. Jim had his arm around her and every little way they stopped and pressed against each other and Jim kissed her. There was no moon and they walked ankle deep in the sandy road through the trees down to the dock and the warehouse on the bay. The water was lapping in the piles and the point was dark across the bay. It was cold but Liz was hot all over from being with Jim. They sat down in the shelter of the warehouse and Jim pulled Liz close to him. She was frightened. One of Jim's hands went inside her dress and stroked over her breast and the other hand was in her lap, She was very frightened and didn't know how he was going to go about things but she snuggled close to him. Then the hand that felt so big in her lap went away and was on her leg and started to move up it.

"Don't Jim." Liz said. Jim slid the hand further up.

"You musn't Jim. You musn't." Neither Jim nor Jim's big hand paid any attention to her.

The boards were hard. Jim had her dress up and was trying to do something to her. She was frightened but she wanted it. She had to have it but it frightened her.

"You musn't do it Jim. You musn't."

"I got to. I'm going to. You know we got to."

"No we haven't Jim. We aint got to. Oh it isn't right. Oh it's so big and it hurts so. You can't. Oh Jim. Jim. Oh."

The hemlock planks of the dock were hard and splintery and cold and Jim was heavy on her and he had hurt her. Liz pushed him, she was so uncomfortable and cramped. Jim was asleep. He wouldn't move. She worked out from under him and sat up and straightened her skirt and coat and tried to do something with her hair. Jim was sleeping with his mouth a little open. Liz leaned over and kissed him on the cheek. He was still asleep. She lifted his head a little and shook it. He rolled his head over and swallowed. Liz started to cry. She walked over to the edge of the dock and looked down to the water. There was a mist coming up from the bay. She was cold and miserable and everything felt gone. She walked back to where Jim was lying and shook him once more to make sure. She was crying.

"Jim" she said, "Jim. Please Jim."

Jim stirred and curled a little tighter. Liz took off her coat and leaned over and covered him with it. She tucked it around him neatly and carefully. Then she walked across the dock and up the steep sandy road to go to bed. A cold mist was coming up through the woods from the bay.

OUT OF SEASON

OUT OF SEASON

ON THE FOUR lira he had earned by spading the hotel garden he got quite drunk. He saw the young gentleman coming down the path and spoke to him mysteriously. The young gentleman said he had not eaten yet but would be ready to go as soon as lunch was finished. Forty minutes or an hour.

At the cantina near the bridge they trusted him for three more grappas because he was so confident and mysterious about his job for the afternoon. It was a windy day with the sun coming out from behind clouds and then going under in sprinkles of rain. A wonderful day for trout fishing.

The young gentleman came out of the hotel and asked him about the rods. Should his wife come behind with the rods? Yes, said Peduzzi, let her follow us. The young gentleman went back into the hotel and spoke to his wife. He and Peduzzi started down the road. The young gentleman had a musette over his shoulder. Peduzzi saw the wife, who looked as young as the young gentleman and was wearing mountain boots and a blue beret, start out to follow them down the road carrying the fishing rods unjointed one in each hand. Peduzzi didn't like her to be way back there. Signorina, he called, winking at the young gentleman, come up here and walk with us. Signora come up here. Let us all walk together. Peduzzi wanted them all three to walk down the street of Cortina together.

The wife stayed behind, following rather sullenly. Signorina, Peduzzi called tenderly, come up here with us. The young gentleman looked back and shouted something. The wife stopped lagging behind and walked up.

Everyone they met walking through the main street of the town Peduzzi greeted elaborately. *Buon' di Arturo!* Tipping his hat. The bank clerk stared at him from the door of the Fascist café. Groups of three and four people standing in front of the shops stared at the three. The workmen in their stone-powdered jackets working on the foundations of the new hotel looked up as they passed. Nobody spoke or gave any sign to them except the town beggar, lean and old with a spittle thickened beard, who lifted his hat as they passed.

Peduzzi stopped in front of a store with the window full of bottles and brought his empty grappa bottle from an inside pocket of his old military coat. A little to drink, some marsala for the Signora, something, something to drink. He gestured with the bottle. It was a wonderful day. Marsala, you like marsala, Signorina? A little marsala?

The wife stood sullenly. You'll have to play up to this, she said. I can't understand a word he says. He's drunk isn't he?

The young gentleman appeared not to hear Peduzzi. He was thinking what in hell makes him say Marsala. That's what Max Beerbohm drinks.

Geld, Peduzzi said finally, taking hold of the young gentleman's sleeve. *Lire*. He smiled reluctant to press the subject but needing to bring the young gentleman into action.

The young gentleman took out his pocket book and gave him a ten lire note. Peduzzi went up the steps to the door of the Speciality of Domestic and Foreign Wines shop. It was locked.

It is closed until two, someone passing in the street said scornfully. Peduzzi came down the steps. He felt hurt. Never mind, he said, we can get it at the Concordia.

They walked down the road to the Concordia three abreast. On the porch of the Concordia where the rusty bobsleds were stacked the young gentleman said, *Was wollen sie?* Peduzzi handed him the ten lira note folded over and over. Nothing, he said, Anything. He was embarrassed. Marsala maybe. I don't know. Marsala?

The door of the Concordia shut on the young gentleman and the wife. Three marsalas, said the y. g. to the girl behind the pastry counter. Two you mean? she asked. No, he said, one for a *vecchio*. Oh, she said, a *vecchio*, and laughed getting down the bottle. She poured out the three muddy looking drinks into three glasses. The wife was sitting at a table under the line of newspapers on sticks. The y. g. put one of the marsalas in front of her. You might as well drink it, he said. Maybe it'll make you feel better. She sat and looked at the glass. The y. g. went outside the door with a glass for Peduzzi but could not see him.

I don't know where he is, he said coming back into the pastry room carrying the glass.

He wanted a quart of it, said the wife.

How much is a quarter litre, the y. g. asked the girl.

Of the bianco? One lira.

No, of the marsala. Put these two in too, he said giving her his own glass and the one poured for Peduzzi. She filled the quarter litre wine measure with a funnel. A bottle to carry it, said the y. g.

She went to hunt for a bottle. It all amused her.

I'm sorry you feel so rotten Tiny, he said, I'm sorry I talked the way I did at lunch. We were both getting at the same thing from different angles.

It doesn't make any difference, she said. None of it makes any difference.

Are you too cold, he asked. I wish you'd worn another sweater.

I've got on three sweaters.

The girl came in with a very slim brown bottle and poured the marsala into it. The y. g. paid five lira more. They went out of the door. The girl was amused. Peduzzi was walking up and down at the other end out of the wind and holding the rods.

Come on, he said, I will carry the rods. What difference does it make if anybody sees them. No one will trouble us. No one will make any trouble for me in Cortina. I know them at the *municipio*. I have been a soldier. Everybody in this town likes me. I sell frogs. What if it is forbidden to fish? Not a thing. Nothing. No trouble. Big trout I tell you. Lots of them.

They were walking down the hill toward the river. The town was in back of them. The sun had gone under and it was sprinkling rain. There, said Peduzzi, pointing to a girl in the doorway of a house they passed. My daughter.

His doctor, the wife said, has he got to show us his doctor?

He said his daughter, said the y. g.

The girl went into the house as Peduzzi pointed.

They walked down the hill across the fields and then turned to follow the river bank. Peduzzi talked rapidly with much winking and knowingness. As they walked three abreast the wife caught his breath across the wind. Once he nudged her in the ribs. Part of the time he talked in D'Ampezzo dialect and sometimes in Tyroler German dialect. He could not make out which the young gentleman and his wife understood the best so he was being bi-lingual. But as the young gentleman said *Ja Ja* Peduzzi decided to talk altogether in Tyroler. The young gentleman and the wife understood nothing.

Everybody in the town saw us going through with these rods. We're probably being followed by the game police now. I wish we weren't in on this damn thing. This damned old fool is so drunk too.

Of course you haven't got the guts to just go back, said the wife. Of course you have to go on.

Why don't you go back? Go on back Tiny.

I'm going to stay with you. If you go to jail we might as well both go.

They turned sharp down the bank and Peduzzi stood his coat blowing in the wind gesturing at the river. It was brown and muddy. Off on the right there was a dump heap.

Say it to me in Italian, said the young gentleman.

Un' mezz' ora. Piu d' un' mezz' ora.

He says it's at least a half an hour more. Go on back Tiny. You're cold in this wind anyway. It's a rotten day and we aren't going to have any fun anyway.

All right, she said, and climbed up the grassy bank.

Peduzzi was down at the river and did not notice her till she was almost out of sight over the crest. Frau! he shouted. Frau! Fraulein! You're not going? She went on over the crest of the hill.

She's gone! said Peduzzi. It shocked him.

He took off the rubber bands that held the rod segments together and commenced to joint up one of the rods.

But you said it was half an hour further.

Oh yes. It is good half an hour down. It is good here too.

Really?

Of course. It is good here and good there too.

The y. g. sat down on the bank and jointed up a rod, put on the reel and threaded the line through the guides. He felt uncomfortable and afraid that any minute a gamekeeper or a posse of citizens would come over the bank from the town. He could see the houses of the town and the campanile over the edge of the hill. He opened his leader box. Peduzzi leaned over and dug his flat hard thumb and forefinger in and tangled the moistened leaders.

Have you some lead?

No.

You must have some lead. Peduzzi was excited. You must have *piombo*. *Piombo*. A little *piombo*. Just here. Just above the hook or your bait will float on the water. You must have it. Just a little *piombo*.

Have you got some?

No. He looked through all his pockets desperately. Sifting through the cloth dirt in the linings of his inside military pockets. I haven't any. We must have *piombo*.

We can't fish then, said the y. g. and unjointed the rod, reeling the line back through the guides. We'll get some *piombo* and fish tomorrow.

But listen *caro*, you must have *piombo*. The line will lie flat on the water. Peduzzi's day was going to pieces before his eyes. You must have *piombo*. A little is enough. Your stuff is all clean and new but you have no lead. I would have brought some. You said you had everything.

The y. g. looked at the stream discoloured by the melting snow. I know, he said, we'll get some *piombo* and fish tomorrow.

At what hour in the morning? Tell me that.

At seven.

The sun came out. It was warm and pleasant. The young gentleman felt relieved. He was no longer breaking the law. Sitting on the bank he took the bottle of marsala out of his pocket and passed it to Peduzzi. Peduzzi passed it back. The y. g. took a drink of it and passed it to Peduzzi again. Peduzzi passed it back again. Drink, he said, drink. It's your marsala. After another short drink the y. g. handed the bottle over. Peduzzi had been watching it closely. He took the bottle very hurriedly and tipped it up. The grey hairs in the folds of his neck oscillated as he drank, his eyes fixed on the end of the narrow brown bottle. He drank it all. The sun shone while he drank. It was wonderful. This was a great day after all. A wonderful day.

Senta caro! In the morning at seven. He had called the young gentleman *caro* several times and nothing had happened. It was good marsala. His eyes glistened. Days like this stretched out ahead. It would begin again at seven in the morning.

They started to walk up the hill toward the town. The y. g. went on ahead. He was quite a way up the hill. Peduzzi called to him.

Listen *caro* can you let me take five lira for a favour?

For today? asked the young gentleman frowning.

No, not today. Give it to me today for tomorrow. I will provide everything for tomorrow. *Pane, salami, formaggio,* good stuff for all of us. You and I and the signora. Bait for fishing, minnows, not worms only. Perhaps I can get some marsala. All for five lira. Five lira for a favour.

The young gentleman looked through his pocket book and took out a two lira note and two ones.

Thank you *caro*. Thank you, said Peduzzi in the tone of one member of the Carleton Club accepting the Morning Post from another. This was living. He was through with the hotel garden, breaking up frozen manure with a dung fork. Life was opening out.

Until seven o'clock then *caro*, he said, slapping the y. g. on the back. Promptly at seven.

I may not be going, said the young gentleman putting his purse back in his pocket.

What, said Peduzzi. I will have minnows Signor. *Salami,* everything. You and I and the Signora. The three of us.

I may not be going, said the y. g., very probably not. I will leave word with the padrone at the hotel office.

MY OLD MAN

MY OLD MAN

I GUESS LOOKING at it now my old man was cut out for a fat guy, one of those regular little roly fat guys you see around, but he sure never got that way, except a little toward the last, and then it wasn't his fault, he was riding over the jumps only and he could afford to carry plenty of weight then. I remember the way he'd pull on a rubber shirt over a couple of jerseys and a big sweat shirt over that and get me to run with him in the forenoon in the hot sun. He'd have maybe taken a trial trip with one of Razzo's skins early in the morning after just getting in from Torino at four o'clock in the morning and beating it out to the stables in a cab and then with the dew all over everything and the sun just starting to get going I'd help him pull off his boots and he'd get into a pair of sneakers and all these sweaters and we'd start out.

"Come on kid" he'd say, stepping up and down on his toes in front of the jock's dressing room, "let's get moving."

Then we'd start off jogging around the infield once maybe with him ahead running nice and then turn out the gate and along one of those roads with all the trees along both sides of them that run out from San Siro. I'd go ahead of him when we hit the road and I could run pretty stout and I'd look around and he'd be jogging easy just behind me and after a little while I'd look around again and he'd begun to sweat. Sweating heavy and he'd just be dogging it along with his eyes on my back, but when he'd catch me looking at him he'd grin and say, "Sweating plenty?" When my old man grinned nobody could help but grin too. We'd keep right on running out toward the mountains and then my old man would yell "Hey Joe!" and I'd look back and he'd be sitting under a tree with a towel he'd had around his waist wrapped around his neck.

I'd come back and sit down beside him and he'd pull a rope out of his pocket and start skipping rope out in the sun with the sweat pouring off his face and him skipping rope out in the white dust with the rope going cloppetty cloppety clop clop clop and the sun hotter and him working harder up and down a patch of the road. Say it was a treat to see my old man skip rope too. He could whirr it fast or lop it slow and fancy. Say you ought to have seen wops look at us sometimes when they'd come by going into town walking along with big white steers hauling the cart. They sure looked as though they thought the old man was nuts. He'd start the rope whirring till they'd stop dead still and watch him, then give the steers a cluck and a poke with the goad and get going again.

When I'd sit watching him working out in the hot sun I sure felt fond of him. He sure was fun and he done his work so hard and he'd finish up with a regular whirring that'd drive the sweat out on his face like water and then sling the rope at the tree and come over and sit down with me and lean back against the tree with the towel and a sweater wrapped around his neck.

"Sure is hell keeping it down, Joe" he'd say and lean back and shut his eyes and breath long and deep, "it aint like when you're a kid." Then he'd get up before he started to cool and we'd jog along back to the stables. That's the way it was keeping down to weight. He was worried all the time. Most jocks can just about ride off all they want to. A jock loses about a kilo every time he rides, but my old man was sort of dried out and he couldn't keep down his kilos without all that running.

I remember once at San Siro, Regoli, a little wop that was riding for Buzoni came out across the paddock going to the bar for something cool and flicking his boots with his whip, after he'd just weighed in and my old man had just weighed in too and came out with the saddle under his arm looking red faced and tired and too big for his silks and he stood there looking at young Regoli standing up to the outdoors bar cool and kid looking and I says, "What's the matter Dad?" cause I thought maybe Regoli had bumped him or something and he just looked at Regoli and said, "Oh to hell with it" and went on to the dressing room.

Well it would have been all right maybe if we'd stayed in Milan and ridden at Milan and Torino cause if there ever were any easy courses it's those two. "Pianola, Joe," my old man said when he dismounted in the winning stall after what the wops thought was a hell of a steeplechase. I asked him once, "This course rides its-self. It's the pace you're going at that makes riding the jumps dangerous Joe. We aint going any pace here, and they aint any really bad jumps either. But it's the pace always—not the jumps that makes the trouble."

San Siro was the swellest course I'd ever seen but the old man said it was a dog's life. Going back and forth between Mirafiore and San Siro and riding just about every day in the week with a train ride every other night.

I was nuts about the horses too. There's something about it when they come out and go up the track to the post. Sort of dancy and tight looking with the jock keeping a tight hold on them and maybe easing off a little and letting them run a little going up. Then once they were at the barrier it got me worse than anything. Especially at San Siro with that big green infield and the mountains way off and the fat wop starter with his big whip and the jocks fiddling them around and then the barrier snapping up and that bell going off and them all getting off in a bunch and then commencing to string out. You know the way a bunch of skins gets off. If you're up in the stand with a pair of glasses all you see is them plunging off and then that bell goes off and it seems like it rings for a thousand years and then they come sweeping round the turn. There wasn't ever anything like it for me.

But my old man said one day in the dressing room when he was getting into his street clothes, "None of these things are horses Joe. They'd kill that bunch of skates for their hides and hoofs up at Paris." That was the day he'd won the Premio Commercio with Lantorna shooting her out of the field the last hundred meters like pulling a cork out of a bottle.

It was right after the Premio Commercio that we pulled out and left Italy. My old man and Holbrook and a fat wop in a straw hat that kept wiping his face with a handkerchief were having an argument at a table in the Galleria. They were all talking French and the two of them were after my old man about something. Finally he didn't say anything any more but just sat there and looked at Holbrook and the two of them kept after him, first one talking and then the other and the fat wop always butting in on Holbrook.

"You go out and buy me a Sportsman, will you Joe?" my old man said and handed me a couple of *soldi* without looking away from Holbrook.

So I went out of the Galleria and walked over to in front of the Scala and bought a paper and came back and stood a little way away because I didn't want to butt in and my old man was sitting back in his chair looking down at his coffee and fooling with a spoon and Holbrook and the big wop were standing and the big wop was wiping his face and shaking his head. And I came up and my old man acted just as though the two of them weren't standing there and said, "Want an ice Joe?" Holbrook looked down at my old man and said slow and careful, "You son of a bitch" and he and the fat wop went out through the tables.

My old man sat there and sort of smiled at me but his face was white and he looked sick as hell and I was scared and felt sick inside because I knew something had happened and I didn't see how anybody could call my old man a son of a bitch and get away with it. My old man opened up the Sportsman and studied the handicaps for a while and then he said, "You got to take a lot of things in this world Joe." And three days later we left Milan for good on the Turin train for Paris after an auction sale out in front of Turner's stables of everything we couldn't get into a trunk and a suit case.

We got into Paris early in the morning in a long dirty station the old man told me was the Gare de Lyon. Paris was an awful big town after Milan. Seems like in Milan everybody is going somewhere and all the trams run somewhere and there aint any sort of a mixup, but Paris is all balled up and they never do straighten it out. I got to like it though, part of it anyway, and say it's got the best race courses in the world. Seems as though that were the thing that keeps it all going and about the only thing you can figure on is that every day the buses will be going out to whatever track they're running at going right out through everything to the track. I never really got to know Paris well because I just came in about once or twice a week with the old man from Maisons and he always sat at the Café de la Paix on the Opera side with the rest of the gang from Maisons and I guess that's one of the busiest parts of the town. But say it is funny that a big town like Paris wouldn't have a Galleria isn't it?

Well, we went out to live at Maisons-Lafitte, where just about everybody lives except the gang at Chantilly, with a Mrs. Meyers that runs a boarding house. Maisons is about the swellest place to live I've ever seen in all my life. The town aint so much, but there's a lake and a swell forest that we used to go off bumming in all day, a couple of us kids, and my old man made me a sling shot and we got a lot of things with it but the best one was a magpie. Young Dick Atkinson shot a rabbit with it one day and we put it under a tree and were all sitting around and Dick had some cigarettes and all of a sudden the rabbit jumped up and beat it into the brush and we chased it but we couldn't find it. Gee we had fun at Maisons. Mrs. Meyers used to give me lunch in the morning and I'd be gone all day. I learned to talk French quick. It's an easy language.

As soon as we got to Maisons my old man wrote to Milan for his license and he was pretty worried till it came. He used to sit around the Café de Paris in Maisons with the gang there, there were lots of guys he'd known when he rode up at Paris before the war lived at Maisons, and there's a lot of time to sit around because the work around a racing stable for the jocks that is, is all cleaned up by nine o'clock in the morning. They take the first batch of skins out to gallop them at 5.30 in the morning and they work the second lot at 8 o'clock. That means getting up early all right and going to bed early too. If a jock's riding for somebody too he can't go boozing around because the trainer always has an eye on him if he's a kid and if he aint a kid he's always got an eye on himself. So mostly if a jock aint working he sits around the Café de Paris with the gang and they can all sit around about two or three hours in front of some drink like a vermouth and seltz and they talk and tell stories and shoot pool and it's sort of like a club or the Galleria in Milan. Only it aint really like the Galleria because there everybody is going by all the time and there's everybody around at the tables.

Well my old man got his license all right. They sent it through to him without a word and he rode a couple of times. Amiens, up country and that sort of thing, but he didn't seem to get any engagement. Everybody liked him and whenever I'd come in to the Café in the forenoon I'd find somebody drinking with him because my old man wasn't tight like most of these jockeys that have got the first dollar they made riding at the World's Fair in St. Louis in Nineteen ought four. That's what my old man would say when he'd kid George Burns. But it seemed like everybody steered clear of giving my old man any mounts.

We went out to wherever they were running every day with the car from Maisons and that was the most fun of all. I was glad when the horses came back from Deauville and the summer. Even though it meant no more bumming in the woods, cause then we'd ride to Enghien or Tremblay or St. Cloud and watch them from the trainers' and jockeys' stand. I sure learned about racing from going out with that gang and the fun of it was going every day.

I remember once out at St. Cloud. It was a big two hundred thousand franc race with seven entries and Kzar a big favourite. I went around to the paddock to see the horses with my old man and you never saw such horses. This Kzar is a great big yellow horse that looks like just nothing but run. I never saw such a horse. He was being led around the paddock with his head down and when he went by me I felt all hollow inside he was so beautiful. There never was such a wonderful, lean, running built horse. And he went around the paddock putting his feet just so and quiet and careful and moving easy like he knew just what he had to do and not jerking and standing up on his legs and getting wild eyed like you see these selling platers with a shot of dope in them. The crowd was so thick I couldn't see him again except just his legs going by and some yellow and my old man started out through the crowd and I followed him over to the jock's dressing room back in the trees and there was a big crowd around there too but the man at the door in a derby nodded to my old man and we got in and everybody was sitting around and getting dressed and pulling shirts over their heads and pulling boots on and it all smelled hot and sweaty and linimenty and outside was the crowd looking in.

The old man went over and sat down beside George Gardner that was getting into his pants and said, "What's the dope George?" just in an ordinary tone of voice cause there aint any use him feeling around because George either can tell him or he can't tell him.

. "He won't win" George says very low, leaning over and buttoning the bottoms of his pants.

"Who will" my old man says leaning over close so nobody can hear.

"Kircubbin" George says, "And if he does, save me a couple of tickets."

My old man says something in a regular voice to George and George says, "Don't ever bet on anything I tell you" kidding like and we beat it out and through all the crowd that was looking in over to the 100 franc mutuel machine. But I knew something big was up because George is Kzar's jockey. On the way he gets one of the yellow odds sheets with the starting prices on and Kzar is only paying 5 for 10, Cefisidote is next at 3 to 1 and fifth down the list this Kircubbin at 8 to 1. My old man bets five thousand on Kircubbin to win and puts on a thousand to place and we went around back of the grandstand to go up the stairs and get a place to watch the race.

We were jammed in tight and first a man in a long coat with a grey tall hat and a whip folded up in his hand came out and then one after another the horses, with the jocks up and a stable boy holding the bridle on each side and walking along, followed the old guy. That big yellow horse Kzar came first. He didn't look so big when you first looked at him until you saw the length of his legs and the whole way he's built and the way he moves. Gosh I never saw such a horse. George Gardner was riding him and they moved along slow, back of the old guy in the gray tall hat that walked along like he was the ring master in a circus. Back of Kzar, moving along smooth and yellow in the sun, was a good looking black with a nice head with Tommy Archibald riding him and after the black was a string of five more horses all moving along slow in a procession past the grandstand and the pesage. My old man said the black was Kircubbin and I took a good look at him and he was a nice looking horse all right but nothing like Kzar.

Everybody cheered Kzar when he went by and he sure was one swell looking horse. The procession of them went around on the other side past the pelouse and then back up to the near end of the course and the circus master had the stable boys turn them loose one after another so they could gallop by the stands on their way up to the post and let everybody have a good look at them. They weren't at the post hardly any time at all when the gong started and you could see them way off across the infield all in a bunch starting on the first swing like a lot of little toy horses. I was watching them through the glasses and Kzar was running well back with one of the bays making the pace. They swept down and around and came pounding past and Kzar was way back when they passed us and this Kircubbin horse in front and going smooth. Gee it's awful when they go by you and then you have to watch them go farther away and get smaller and smaller and then all bunched up on the turns and then come around towards into the stretch and you feel like swearing and goddaming worse and worse. Finally they made the last turn and came into the straightaway with this Kircubbin horse way out in front. Everybody was looking funny and saying "Kzar" in sort of a sick way and they pounding nearer down the stretch, and then something came out of the pack right into my glasses like a horse-headed yellow streak and everybody began to yell "Kzar" as though they were crazy. Kzar came on

faster than I'd ever seen anything in my life and pulled up on
Kircubbin that was going fast as any black horse could go with
the jock flogging hell out of him with the gad and they were
right dead neck and neck for a second but Kzar seemed going
about twice as fast with those great jumps and that head out—
but it was while they were neck and neck that they passed the
winning post and when the numbers went up in the slots the
first one was 2 and that meant Kircubbin had won.

I felt all trembly and funny inside, and then we were all
jammed in with the people going down stairs to stand in front
of the board where they'd post what Kircubbin paid. Honest
watching the race I'd forgot how much my old man had bet on
Kircubbin. I'd wanted Kzar to win so damned bad. But now it
was all over it was swell to know we had the winner.

"Wasn't it a swell race Dad?" I said to him.

He looked at me sort of funny with his derby on the back of
his head, "George Gardner's a swell jockey all right," he said, "It
sure took a great jock to keep that Kzar horse from winning."

Of course I knew it was funny all the time. But my old man
saying that right out like that sure took the kick all out of it for
me and I didn't get the real kick back again ever, even when
they posted the numbers up on the board and the bell rang to
pay off and we saw that Kircubbin paid 67.50 for 10. All around
people were saying "Poor Kzar. Poor Kzar!" And I thought,
I wish I were a jockey and could have rode him instead of that
son of a bitch. And that was funny, thinking of George Gardner
as a son of a bitch because I'd always liked him and besides he'd
given us the winner, but I guess that's what he is all right.

My old man had a big lot of money after that race and he
took to coming into Paris oftener. If they raced at Tremblay
he'd have them drop him in town on their way back to Maisons
and he and I'd sit out in front of the Café de la Paix and watch
the people go by. It's funny sitting there. There's streams of

people going by and all sorts of guys come up and want to sell you things and I loved to sit there with my old man. That was when we'd have the most fun. Guys would come by selling funny rabbits that jumped if you squeezed a bulb and they'd come up to us and my old man would kid with them. He could talk French just like English and all those kind of guys knew him cause you can always tell a jockey—and then we always sat at the same table and they got used to seeing us there. There were guys selling matrimonial papers and girls selling rubber eggs that when you squeezed them a rooster came out of them and one old wormy looking guy that went by with post cards of Paris showing them to everybody, and of course nobody ever bought any and then he would come back and show the under side of the pack and they would all be smutty post cards and lots of people would dig down and buy them.

Gee I remember the funny people that used to go by. Girls around supper time looking for somebody to take them out to eat and they'd speak to my old man and he'd make some joke at them in French and they'd pat me on the head and go on. Once there was an American woman sitting with her kid daughter at the next table to us and they were both eating ices and I kept looking at the girl and she was awfully good looking and I smiled at her and she smiled at me but that was all that ever came of it because I looked for her mother and her every day and I made up ways that I was going to speak to her and I wondered if I got to know her if her mother would let me take her out to Auteuil or Tremblay but I never saw either of them again. Anyway I guess it wouldn't have been any good anyway because looking back on it I remember the way I thought out would be best to speak to her was to say, "Pardon me, but perhaps I can give you a winner at Enghien today?" and after all maybe she would have thought I was a tout instead of really trying to give her a winner.

We'd sit at the Café de la Paix, my old man and me, and we had a big drag with the waiter because my old man drank whisky and it cost five francs and that meant a good tip when the saucers were counted up. My old man was drinking more than I'd ever seen him, but he wasn't riding at all now and besides he said that whiskey kept his weight down. But I noticed he was putting it on all right just the same. He'd busted away from his old gang out at Maisons and seemed to like just sitting around on the boulevard with me. But he was dropping money every day at the track. He'd feel sort of doleful after the last race, if he'd lost on the day, until we'd get to our table and he'd have his first whiskey and then he'd be fine.

He'd be reading the Paris-Sport and he'd look over at me and say, "Where's your girl Joe?" to kid me on account I had told him about the girl that day at the next table. And I'd get red but I liked being kidded about her. It gave me a good feeling. "Keep your eye peeled for her Joe," he'd say, "She'll be back."

He'd ask me questions about things and some of the things I'd say he'd laugh. And then he'd get started talking about things. About riding down in Egypt, or at St. Moritz on the ice before my mother died, and about during the war when they had regular races down in the south of France without any purses, or betting or crowd or anything just to keep the breed up. Regular races with the jocks riding hell out of the horses. Gee I could listen to my old man talk by the hour, especially when he'd had a couple or so of drinks. He'd tell me about when he was a boy in Kentucky and going coon hunting and the old days in the states before everything went on the bum there. And he'd say, "Joe, when we've got a decent stake, you're going back there to the States and go to school."

"What've I got to go back there to go to school for when everything's on the bum there?" I'd ask him.

"That's different." he'd say and get the waiter over and pay the pile of saucers and we'd get a taxi to the Gare St. Lazare and get on the train out to Maisons.

One day at Auteuil after a selling steeplechase my old man bought in the winner for 30.000 francs. He had to bid a little to get him but the stable let the horse go finally and my old man had his permit and his colors in a week. Gee I felt proud when my old man was an owner. He fixed it up for stable space with Charles Drake and cut out coming in to Paris and started his running and sweating out again and him and I were the whole stable gang. Our horse's name was Gillford, he was Irish bred and a nice sweet jumper. My old man figured that training him and riding him himself he was a good investment. I was proud of everything and I thought Gillford was as good a horse as Kzar. He was a good solid jumper, a bay, with plenty of speed on the flat if you asked him for it and he was a nice looking horse too.

Gee I was fond of him. The first time he started with my old man up he finished third in a 2.500 meter hurdle race and when my old man got off him, all sweating and happy in the place stall and went in to weigh I felt as proud of him as though it was the first race he'd ever placed in. You see when a guy aint been riding for a long time you can't make yourself really believe that he has ever rode. The whole thing was different now cause down in Milan even big races never seemed to make any difference to my old man, if he won he wasn't ever excited or anything, and now it was so I couldn't hardly sleep the night before a race and I knew my old man was excited too even if he didn't show it. Riding for yourself makes an awful difference.

Second time Gillford and my old man started was a rainy Sunday at Auteuil in the Prix du Marat, a 4.500 meter steeplechase. As soon as he'd gone out I beat it up in the stand with the new glasses my old man had bought for me to watch them.

They started way over at the far end of the course and there was
some trouble at the barrier. Something with goggle blinders on
was making a great fuss and rearing around and busted the bar-
rier once but I could see my old man in our black jacket with
a white cross and a black cap sitting up on Gillford and patting
him with his hand. Then they were off in a jump and out of
sight behind the trees and the gong going for dear life and the
pari mutuel wickets rattling down. Gosh I was so excited I was
afraid to look at them but I fixed the glasses on the place where
they would come out back of the trees and then out they came
with the old black jacket going third and they all sailing over
the jump like birds. Then they went out of sight again and then
they came pounding out and down the hill and all going nice
and sweet and easy and taking the fence smooth in a bunch and
moving away from us all solid. Looked as though you could
walk across on their backs they were all so bunched and going
so smooth, Then they bellied over the big double Bullfinch and
something came down. I couldn't see who it was but in a
minute the horse was up and galloping free and the field, all
bunched still, sweeping around the long left turn into the
straightaway. They jumped the stone wall and came jammed
down the stretch toward the big water jump right in front of
the stands. I saw them coming and hollered at my old man as
he went by and he was leading by about a length and riding
way out over and light as a monkey and they were racing for
the water jump. They took off over the big hedge of the water
jump in a pack and then there was a crash and two horses pulled
sideways out off it and kept on going and three others were
piled up. I couldn't see my old man anywhere. One horse
knee-ed himself up and the jock had hold of the bridle and
mounted and went slamming on after the place money. The
other horse was up and away by himself, jerking his head and
galloping with the bridle rein hanging and the jock staggered

over to one side of the track against the fence. Then Gillford rolled over to one side off my old man and got up and started to run on three legs with his off hoof dangling and there was my old man lying there on the grass flat out with his face up and blood all over the side of his head. I ran down the stand and bumped into a jam of people and got to the rail and a cop grabbed me and held me and two big stretcher bearers were going out after my old man and around on the other side of the course I saw three horses, strung way out, coming out of the trees and taking the jump.

My old man was dead when they brought him in and while a doctor was listening to his heart with a thing plugged in his ears I heard a shot up the track that meant they'd killed Gillford. I lay down beside my old man when they carried the stretcher into the hospital room and hung onto the stretcher and cried and cried and he looked so white and gone and so awfully dead and I couldn't help feeling that if my old man was dead maybe they didn't need to have shot Gillford. His hoof might have got well. I don't know. I loved my old man so much.

Then a couple of guys came in and one of them patted me on the back and then went over and looked at my old man and then pulled a sheet off the cot and and spread it over him; and the other was telephoning in French for them to send the ambulance to take him out to Maisons. And I couldn't stop crying, crying and choking, sort of, and George Gardner came in and sat down beside me on the floor and put his arm around me and says, "Come on Joe old boy. Get up and we'll go out and wait for the ambulance."

George and I went out to the gate and I was trying to stop bawling and George wiped off my face with his handkerchief and we were standing back a little ways while the crowd was going out of the gate and a couple of guys stopped near us while we were waiting for the crowd to get through the gate and one of them was counting a bunch of mutuel tickets and he said, "Well Butler got his all right."

The other guy said, "I don't give a good goddam if he did, the crook. He had it coming to him on the stuff he's pulled."

"I'll say he had," said the other guy and tore the bunch of tickets in two.

And George Gardner looked at me to see if I'd heard and I had all right and he said, "Don't you listen to what those bums said Joe. Your old man was one swell guy."

But I don't know. Seems like when they get started they don't leave a guy nothing.

TEN POEMS

MITRAIGLIATRICE

The mills of the gods grind slowly;
But this mill
Chatters in mechanical staccato.
Ugly short infantry of the mind,
Advancing over difficult terrain,
Make this Corona
Their mitrailleuse.

OKLAHOMA

All of the Indians are dead
(a good Indian is a dead Indian)
Or riding in motor cars—
(the oil lands, you know, they're all rich)
Smoke smarts my eyes,
Cottonwood twigs and buffalo dung
Smoke grey in the teepee—
(or is it myopic trachoma)

The prairies are long,
The moon rises,
Ponies
Drag at their pickets.
The grass has gone brown in the summer—
(or is it the hay crop failing)

Pull an arrow out:
If you break it
The wound closes.
Salt is good too
And wood ashes.
Pounding it throbs in the night—
(or is it the gonorrhea)

OILY WEATHER

The sea desires deep hulls—
It swells and rolls.
The screw churns a throb—
Driving, throbbing, progressing.
The sea rolls with love
Surging, caressing,
Undulating its great loving belly.
The sea is big and old—
Throbbing ships scorn it.

ROOSEVELT

Workingmen believed
He busted trusts,
And put his picture in their windows.
"What he'd have done in France!"
They said.
Perhaps he would—
He could have died
Perhaps,
Though generals rarely die except in bed,
As he did finally.
And all the legends that he started in his life
Live on and prosper,
Unhampered now by his existence.

CAPTIVES

Some came in chains
Unrepentent but tired.
Too tired but to stumble.
Thinking and hating were finished
Thinking and fighting were finished
Retreating and hoping were finished.
Cures thus a long campaign,
Making death easy.

CHAMPS D'HONNEUR

Soldiers never do die well;
    Crosses mark the places—
Wooden crosses where they fell,
    Stuck above their faces.
Soldiers pitch and cough and twitch—
    All the world roars red and black;
Soldiers smother in a ditch,
    Choking through the whole attack.

RIPARTO D'ASSALTO

Drummed their boots on the camion floor,
Hob-nailed boots on the camion floor.
Sergeants stiff,
Corporals sore.
Lieutenant thought of a Mestre whore—
Warm and soft and sleepy whore,
Cozy, warm and lovely whore;
Damned cold, bitter, rotten ride,
Winding road up the Grappa side.
Arditi on benches stiff and cold,
Pride of their country stiff and cold,
Bristly faces, dirty hides—
Infantry marches, Arditi rides.
Grey, cold, bitter, sullen ride—
To splintered pines on the Grappa side
At Asalone, where the truck-load died.

MONTPARNASSE

There are never any suicides in the quarter among
                              people one knows
No successful suicides.
A Chinese boy kills himself and is dead.
(they continue to place his mail in the letter rack
at the Dome)
A Norwegian boy kills himself and is dead.
(no one knows where the other Norwegian boy has
                                                gone)
They find a model dead
alone in bed and very dead.
(it made almost unbearable trouble for the concierge)
Sweet oil, the white of eggs, mustard and water,
                                          soap suds
and stomach pumps rescue the people one knows.
Every afternoon the people one knows can be found
                                          at the Café.

ALONG WITH YOUTH

A porcupine skin,
Stiff with bad tanning,
It must have ended somewhere.
Stuffed horned owl
Pompous
Yellow eyed;
Chuck-wills-widow on a biassed twig
Sooted with dust.
Piles of old magazines,
Drawers of boy's letters
And the line of love
They must have ended somewhere.
Yesterday's Tribune is gone
Along with youth
And the canoe that went to pieces on the beach
The year of the big storm
When the hotel burned down
At Seney, Michigan.

CHAPTER HEADING

For we have thought the longer thoughts
    And gone the shorter way.
And we have danced to devils' tunes,
    Shivering home to pray;
To serve one master in the night,
    Another in the day.